Henry Flagler, Builder of Florida

Florida East Coast Railway, Key West Extension, Express Train crossing Famous Long Key Viaduct, Florida.

Henry Flagler's East Coast Railway ran all the way from Jacksonville through the Florida Keys by the end of his life. His railroad brought big changes to Florida.
(Courtesy of the State Archives of Florida)

Henry Flagler, Builder of Florida

Sandra Wallus Sammons

Pineapple Press, Inc.

Sarasota, Florida

To Carol Ulgener, who encouraged me to write about the inspiring people in Florida's history, and to my son David Sammons, who totally enjoys living in the Sunshine State.

Pineapple Press, Inc.
P.O. Box 3889
Sarasota, Florida 34230

www.pineapplepress.com

Library of Congress Cataloging-in-Publication Data

Sammons, Sandra Wallus.
Henry Flagler, builder of Florida / Sandra Wallus Sammons. – 1st ed.
    p. cm.
Includes bibliographical references and index.
ISBN 978-1-56164-466-7 (hardback : alk. paper) – ISBN 978-1-56164-467-4
(pbk.: alk. paper)
1. Flagler, Henry Morrison, 1830–1913—Juvenile literature. 2. Florida—
Biography—Juvenile literature. 3. Industrialists—United States—Biography—
Juvenile literature. 4. Businessmen—United States—Biography—Juvenile
literature. 5. Capitalists and financiers—United States—Biography—Juvenile
literature. 6. Florida—History—1865—Juvenile literature. 7. Railroads—
Florida—History—Juvenile literature. I. Title.

F316.F56S26 2010
975.9'06092—dc22
[B]
                                                            2010006030

First Edition
Hb: 10 9 8 7 6 5 4 3 2 1
Pb: 10 9 8 7 6 5 4 3 2

Design by Shé Hicks
Printed in the United States of America

Contents

Florida East Coast Railway,
Key West Extension,
Train crossing
Bahia Honda Bridge, Florida

Henry Flagler's Florida East Coast Railway train rolls toward Key West. (Courtesy of the State Archives of Florida)

Foreword

Henry Morrison Flagler made his first trip to Florida because of his wife's health. Henry and Mary Flagler lived in New York, where winter weather usually brought freezing temperatures. Their doctors told them that Mary needed to spend her winters in a warmer climate.

The Southern state of Florida seldom had freezing temperatures. However, in 1878, Florida was hard to reach. Northern states like New York had cities and roads and even some railroads. Florida, though, had mostly small settlements and many deep woods, mosquitoes, and alligators. With no cars and very few railroads back in those days, visitors traveled by horseback, bumpy stagecoach, or by boats along the state's dangerous coastline.

The few railroads in Florida usually went for short

distances, and most did not connect with the Northern states.

Henry Flagler made his second trip to Florida several years later. This time he saw more than problems. He saw the potential, the possibilities, in the state. On his third visit he decided to build a grand hotel in the city of St. Augustine.

After building the Hotel Ponce de Leon, one project led to another. In order to get people to his hotels, Henry Flagler needed to improve railroads that others had built. He also went on to build some of his own. His railroads brought many people to the east coast of Florida, from Jacksonville all the way to the Florida Keys. Towns grew into cities. People began to come not only to visit during the cold Northern winters, but to stay and make Florida their home.

At about the same time, Henry Bradley Plant was opening up central and southwest Florida for development. The two Henrys were friendly competitors as they tried to build the biggest and best hotels. They opened up a state that was ready for their ideas and their money. While they were at it, both men enjoyed themselves.

The story of Henry Morrison Flagler is an important, and exciting, part of Florida's history.

I have always been contented, but I have never been satisfied. To be dissatisfied means that you are ambitious to progress, to do things, not that you may be richer, but that you may be useful and take a part in the work of the world.
—Henry Morrison Flagler

Chapter 1

Young Henry Flagler

As a young man, Henry Morrison Flagler made a decision never to be poor again. His parents had little money even to feed the family when he was born in New York on January 2, 1830. When he finished the eighth grade in school, Henry knew it was time to leave home. The quiet but determined young man convinced his mother and father that he could take care of himself. He went off to Ohio to make his own way in the world.

His mother was not too worried. She knew that he would be with family. Henry's older half-brother, Daniel Harkness, was working at his uncle's general store in the town of Republic, Ohio. Henry had been invited to work with him.

The trip, however, was a challenge for a fourteen-year-old. It was a chilly autumn day when Henry said goodbye to his parents. He walked nine miles to reach a port where he could take a boat going west. With him he carried a small bag that held all of his possessions.

To pay his fare for the trip, Henry worked as one of the crew on the boat to Buffalo, New York. Taking a second boat from Buffalo to Sandusky, Ohio, he was able to pay his way. The ride was very rough, and the young man got seasick. His legs were wobbly when he finally reached land again. He rested for a short time to get the strength back in his legs. He still had many miles to walk to reach Dan's house. He bravely made the whole trip alone. When he arrived safely, Henry sighed with relief. He had only a French coin, a nickel, and four pennies left in his pocket.

Young Flagler received a warm welcome from Dan and his family. The very next day, he started work at L. G. Harkness and Company. Henry began as a clerk six days a week doing many different jobs around the store. His salary was five dollars a month plus room and board. He saved every penny. After all, he remembered his promise to himself that he would never again be without enough money. He even chose not to buy a blanket during the cold Ohio winter. Instead, he pulled wrapping paper over himself for extra warmth while he slept.

Henry quickly learned the rules of being

successful in business. He worked long hours. If he
made a mistake, he made sure he learned from it.
On Sundays or in the evenings, Henry did not go
celebrating with his friends. He didn't want to spend the
money. Besides, he was exhausted from all his hours of
work.

His dedication to his job was noticed. After five
years, Henry was asked to go to work at another store
Dan's uncle owned. He agreed, even though it meant
he had to move from Republic to Bellevue, Ohio.
At his new job, he earned more than thirty dollars a
month. Mr. Harkness must have been very pleased with
Henry's work!

Mr. Harkness' pretty daughter Mary was also
happy that Henry had moved to Bellevue. She enjoyed
being with Henry and they soon fell in love. Henry
Flagler and Mary Harkness were married in November
of 1853. They had three children. Henry continued to
be careful with the money he earned. Soon he was able
to go into business for himself.

Henry tried different kinds of businesses. Some
were successful and some were not. It was when he
became partners with a friend that he became very rich.
He and John D. Rockefeller made a fortune in refining
oil in Ohio. Henry explained: "We worked night and

Henry Flagler with his wife Mary (in back) and Mary's sister Isabelle, photo dated in the 1850s. (Courtesy of the State Archives of Florida)

day, making good oil as cheaply as possible and selling it for all we could get."

Henry M. Flagler and John D. Rockefeller worked hard at their business. They also bought other, smaller companies that were refining oil. Their company became the largest oil business in America: the

Henry Morrison Flagler at 40 years of age. (Courtesy of the State Archives of Florida)

Standard Oil Company. Henry M. Flagler and John D. Rockefeller became millionaires. Henry had kept the promise he had made to himself. He would never again have to worry about money.

Chapter 2

Trips to the South

The Flagler family moved east when Standard Oil Company set up its main offices in New York City. Henry still worked long hours. Each evening, however, he enjoyed quiet time reading to his much-loved wife, Mary. She had never been in very good health. In 1877, Mary became quite sick. Her doctors said she should spend the coldest part of the winter in a warmer climate. Henry was very busy at his growing business. But he also cared deeply about his wife's health. So when the cold weather came, the Flagler family went South.

There were not many people in Florida when the Flaglers first visited the state. Some people had settled in north Florida. The land there was good for starting farms or other businesses. But not many people had settled in central and south Florida. This was because of the land, the weather, and the wildness there. A lot of the land was either too wet or too dry. The weather was very hot, especially in the summer. Sometimes there were even hurricanes. There were snakes, mosquitoes, and alligators in the miles of deep woods. And, with very little transportation available in Florida then, people did not have many ways to get to south Florida.

The Flagler family arrived in Jacksonville, Florida, in the winter of 1878. The weather was pleasant, and Mary had a good rest. But there was nothing much to do. There were no large hotels. And there were no good roads for traveling to other parts of the state.

After a few weeks, Henry made plans to return to New York. He was needed back at the quickly-growing Standard Oil Company. Although it was best for Mary to stay in the warm weather, she would not stay without her husband. The next winter, Henry again encouraged Mary to return to Florida, but she chose to stay in New York with him. Henry Flagler went on making huge amounts of money. Then, in 1881, his life changed.

Mary Harkness Flagler died. Henry lost his beloved wife.

Suddenly all the money he had made didn't seem so important. Flagler went through a time of deep pain and grief. But then he realized he must get on with his life. Flagler knew he had to get his mind off his loss. To do that, he decided to concentrate on something entirely new.

His friend, Henry Plant, was buying and building railroads in central and western Florida, helping to bring better transportation there. Flagler was already investing in Plant's railroads. Articles in Northern newspapers told of how the Florida government was even giving away land in exchange for anyone willing to build railroads in the state. Flagler decided to visit Florida again. Maybe Florida was a more interesting place to visit than he had thought on his last trip.

In December of 1883, Henry traveled south with his new wife, Ida Alice Shourds Flagler. It still took many days to travel by train from New York to Jacksonville. After a short rest in Jacksonville, Henry and Ida Alice left for St. Augustine.

Ida Alice Shourds Flagler, Henry's second wife. (© *Flagler Museum Archives)*

Chapter 3

A Closer Look at Florida

The trip farther south was a pleasant one. They boarded a steamboat headed south along the beautiful St. Johns River to the little town of Tocoi. On the relaxing trip, they saw many trees loaded with oranges, grapefruit, lemons, and limes. The smell of flowers in bloom was a pleasant change from the winter weather they had just left. Birds and wildlife were everywhere.

When they reached the landing at Tocoi, they took the little St. Johns Railway into St. Augustine. The fifteen-mile ride was bumpy and slow. The St. Johns Railway cars at that time were pulled by an engine, but just a short time before, they had been pulled by horses.

The Flaglers enjoyed their visit. There were no large hotels in St. Augustine, but it was still a delightful place to spend some time. History was important to the people living there because it was the oldest

The St. Johns Railway when it was pulled by horses. (Courtesy of the State Archives of Florida)

permanently settled city in the United States. The old Spanish-style buildings were certainly different from what the Flaglers were used to seeing in New York. Palm trees and flowers were everywhere. It was almost March of 1884 before they left, and the Flaglers had already made plans to return.

The next winter, the weather forecast in New York was for snow and cold. Ida Alice and Henry again boarded a train to go south. This time, however, the trip was not so long, and not so tiring. More railroad track had been built connecting New York and Florida. And Henry had his own private railroad car!

The couple traveled comfortably from New York to Florida in February of 1885. They arrived in Jacksonville in just two days. They stayed only a short time because Henry was anxious to get back to St. Augustine. He wanted to see a new hotel there, called the San Marco. He also wanted to see what else was new in the old city.

There was still no bridge across the St. Johns River, so the Flaglers left their private railroad car at Jacksonville and took a boat across to the south shore. At south Jacksonville, they took the Jacksonville, St. Augustine & Halifax River Railway to the gates of St. Augustine.

When they arrived, Henry Flagler was happy to see many changes. The San Marco was beautiful, and the Flaglers were made very comfortable in their rooms there. Henry also noticed other new buildings being constructed and other wealthy people from the North coming to visit the old city. St. Augustine was no longer a sleepy little town thinking of its past. It had become a busy little city looking toward a successful future. Henry and Ida Alice enjoyed their visit so much that they stayed longer than they had planned.

In March, the people of St. Augustine held a special celebration in honor of the discovery of Florida in 1513 by Ponce de León. Henry Flagler noticed the enthusiasm of the people. He made a decision. He would help the growth of the little town. He would build a hotel in St. Augustine and name it the Hotel Ponce de Leon.

That decision changed his life and Florida's future.

Henry and Ida Alice left St. Augustine on April 1, 1885, but Henry made plans to return in May with a business adviser and an architect. Someone asked why this businessman who had built up an oil company would want to build a hotel. Henry Flagler answered: "For about fourteen or fifteen years, I have devoted my time exclusively to business, and now I am pleasing myself."

And please himself he did. Henry, at fifty-four years old, was at the age when many men would be preparing for retirement. But instead, he was about to start something totally new.

Chapter 4

Building in St. Augustine

Henry Flagler told his architects to design a spectacular Spanish-style hotel. He did not worry about the cost. He was still making a lot of money from the Standard Oil Company. Workmen started digging in December of 1885, and they finished building two years later. When the Hotel Ponce de Leon opened its doors in January of 1888, guests were fascinated by the huge building.

Walking through the rooms, they saw beautiful carved wood and paintings on the walls. Windows of stained glass reflected multi-colored light on the elegant furniture. Even the door knobs were unusual. They were shaped to look like sea shells! There were tall towers on the building and cool, bubbling fountains in the gardens. The entire hotel had a look of comfort and luxury. The cost of the Ponce de Leon was $2,500,000. It was filled with people as soon as it opened.

The fabulous Hotel Ponce de Leon, St. Augustine, Florida. (Courtesy of the State Archives of Florida)

Henry Flagler did not stop at one hotel. Even before the first was finished, he built the Alcazar across the street. The Alcazar charged less for its rooms, but was still very comfortable. And to the surprise of the people living in the city, Mr. Flagler then bought a *third* hotel, the Casa Monica. He renamed it the Cordova.

Now there were three marvelous hotels, as well as a railroad connecting St. Augustine to south Jacksonville. St. Augustine became a good vacation choice for many people. Some guests enjoyed the city so much that they bought land and settled there. Mr. Flagler's hotels had changed St. Augustine. The quiet little town was suddenly a thriving city!

Henry did even more for St. Augustine. He

wanted the town to be as modern and as comfortable as possible for his guests and the residents, so he helped pay for schools and churches in the city. The electric light had been invented, and Mr. Flagler helped to bring electricity to the town. This delighted many of the townspeople. He also built an elegant house for himself and his wife, which they called Kirkside.

He did not stop there. Another challenge presented itself. Henry Flagler may not have planned on also getting into the railroad business, but he soon had to consider that as well. His hotel builders found it hard to get supplies on time because both boat and railroad transportation into St. Augustine were slow and unreliable. Henry also realized that his guests wanted to travel in comfort while coming to the city. He made an appointment to talk with the owners of the little railroad from south Jacksonville.

The best way to improve the railroad line was to buy it and do the job himself. At the end of December 1885, Flagler owned the Jacksonville, St. Augustine & Halifax River Railway. He had workers start on improvements right away. Railroad cars and track were updated to make them faster and more reliable. Later, a bridge was built across the St. Johns River.

When Henry Flagler started a project, he did

his very best to make sure the job was done not only correctly, but also completely. He took the next step, buying two other small lines, the St. Johns Railway and the St. Augustine & Palatka Railway. Those railroad tracks connected the town with the St. Johns River and the steamboats there.

There were three railroads coming to St. Augustine. There were also three hotels for guests to enjoy. All of this was owned by Henry Flagler! The city continued to grow.

In 1889, Henry Flagler received some very sad news. His daughter, Jennie Louise Flagler Benedict, had given birth to a baby girl, but the baby died soon after she was born. Jennie Louise then also became sick and died. Henry had loved his daughter very much and was extremely saddened by this loss. In her memory, he built the beautiful Memorial Presbyterian Church in St. Augustine.

Chapter 5

Going Farther South

Henry Morrison Flagler had changed an entire city. Would a man with so much energy and passion stop there?

He knew what a difference he had made in St. Augustine. He knew that he had enjoyed the challenge. And he also knew that there were small groups of people living in towns south of there that could use good railroad service.

There already was another railway built through the deep woods. Starting in East Palatka, the railway was used by loggers who were cutting wood in the area. The line ended at Daytona, about fifty miles farther south, on the Atlantic Ocean.

Since Henry's St. Augustine & Palatka Railway ended where the logging railroad began, he saw an easy way to extend his tracks south. He knew that it would

Jacksonville, St. Augustine & Halifax River passenger train along Florida's east coast. (Courtesy of the State Archives of Florida)

also be used by farmers and other settlers along its route. Henry bought the line.

He updated the track and the cars. Then he found that cows and wild animals constantly tried to walk across the tracks. He had a wire fence built on both sides of the track almost all the way from south Jacksonville to Daytona. With that done, trains ran on a regular schedule, and Daytona, too, started to grow into a city.

What was next? His friend, Henry Plant, was buying and building railroads on the west coast of Florida, connecting small towns there to cities in Northern states. He was also making it easier for people to come to Florida to live. Henry Flagler looked again to the south. He knew that adventurous people had started other small settlements farther along the east coast. Those people could use better land transportation.

Farmers along the Indian River in Florida were growing mouth-watering oranges and pineapples, and they wanted to sell them in the North. But to get the fruit there, they first needed to ship it by boat to Jacksonville. Then it still had to go by train to Northern cities. That was too slow. The fruit was sometimes overripe and rotten before it arrived. Those farmers needed a train to carry their fruit straight through to markets in the North.

Henry Flagler had to learn a lot before going farther south. He had been buying railroads that had already been built. The woods had already been cleared by someone else. But there were no railroads to buy south of Daytona. There were only unexplored forests and marshy wetlands. There were also many, many snakes and alligators that did not want to be disturbed.

A Florida rattlesnake ready to strike. (Courtesy of the State Archives of Florida)

He and his advisers considered what to do. Henry took a boat trip south along the coast.

Henry visited a small settlement at Lake Worth, in the area that now also includes Palm Beach and West Palm Beach. Only about twelve families were living there at the time, but he realized that many others would love to visit this paradise. The beauty of the land and water was breathtaking. Gentle breezes blew in off the Atlantic Ocean. Palms decorated the miles of beaches. The clear waters of Lake Worth were surrounded by colorful tropical plants, flowering vines, and the awesome royal poinciana, a delicate, umbrella-shaped tree that has beautiful scarlet and orange flowers.

Henry spoke with some of the settlers. He found that they would be happy for him to build another of his grand hotels in the middle of all this splendor!

He made his decision. He would continue his railroad line south and build another hotel. Since Flagler was sixty-three years old then, many people thought that the Lake Worth area would be the terminus, or last stop, of his railroad line.

Other businessmen paid attention to Henry Flagler's decisions about going farther with his railroad track. When they knew it was certain he would build as far south as the Lake Worth area, they immediately bought land near there. They knew that the prices of any land along the track would go up and that they would be able to sell it for a lot more money once the railroad came. They had seen and heard what Henry had done for St. Augustine. They knew that the beautiful little area would soon be booming. All it needed was a man with ideas and the money to put them into effect.

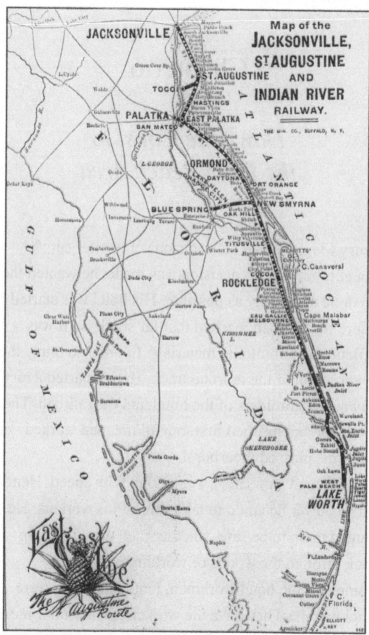

A map of Henry Flagler's railway before it became known as the Florida East Coast Railway. Over the years, Flagler's railroad continued down Florida's east coast. (Courtesy of the State Archives of Florida)

Chapter 6

✹

Down the Coast to the Palm Beach Area

Henry Flagler made his decisions only after careful thought, but when a decision was made, he wanted the job done as quickly as possible. His hotel was started before the railroad reached that far south, so it was difficult to get building materials. In order to hurry the construction of the railroad track, Henry started a race between the builders of the hotel and the railroad. The hotel workers finished first, but all the men worked very fast. This pleased their boss!

Thoughts of safety went along with speed. Henry did whatever he could to take care of his workers. He wanted them to be safe, whether they were building track through the woods or working on a hotel. Homes for the hotel workmen, tents or shacks, were quickly built. They gave the workers shelter until more permanent homes could be built, but there was always the danger of a fire. Henry set up a fire department, and the firefighters were called the "Flagler Alerts." A bell at City Hall was used to call them in case of fire.

There were no cars or trucks at that time, so the kind of fire engine we have these days was not available. When the "Alerts" heard the ringing of the bell, they would jump on their bicycles and pedal as fast as they could to the City Hall. There they put on helmets and coats, and then they rushed to the fire with a hand pump and hose on a cart. The "Alerts" could only hope that the fire would not be out of control by the time they got there.

Henry's hotel would again be spectacular, even larger than the Hotel Ponce de Leon. When finished, it was six stories tall. His hotel was taller than all the buildings nearby.

The Hotel Royal Poinciana opened in February of 1894, and Henry's guests were again amazed. The outside of the large wooden building was painted yellow, reflecting the bright Florida sunshine. On the inside, there were more than 500 bedrooms, and a dining room that employed over 300 waiters! As soon as the railroad was finished being built to Lake Worth, guests packed the hotel during the winter season. Henry Flagler had another successful hotel. He had also brought railroad track farther south along the east coast of Florida.

The Royal Poinciana faced Lake Worth. It was so popular that Flagler also built a second hotel nearby overlooking the Atlantic Ocean. It was first named the Palm Beach Inn, but later called The Breakers. It is still in use as an elegant hotel to this day.

Lake Worth was the terminus, or end, of the Flagler Railroad then. Still, people could not stop asking the big question. Would Henry Flagler go even farther south along the east coast with his railroad?

Royal Poinciana.
(Courtesy of the State Archives of Florida)

Chapter 7

Problems Along the Way

Henry had successes in Florida, but he also had some problems. Most of the state is so far south that it seldom gets freezing temperatures, but that doesn't mean it never does. Advertisements in the North hoping to bring people to Florida told of sunshine and warmth, but during the winter of 1894–1895, much of the state got very cold. Freezing air from the north blew as far south as the Palm Beach area. Citrus and vegetable crops that were ready for market were destroyed. Many people were taken by surprise and began to wonder if Florida really was a good place to live. Some settlers packed up all they had and left.

Henry Flagler thought of ways to help the farmers. He did not want them to be without food or jobs, and he did not want them to leave Florida. He had built hotels

An orange grove after freezing weather, 1895. (Courtesy of the State Archives of Florida)

and railroads. He needed cities and farms to grow, not disappear!

He asked the engineers of his trains to sound their whistles should another freeze be predicted. At least that would give the farmers some warning. They would have some time to try to protect their crops and trees from the frost.

He made loans to farmers, including one owner of a large orange grove along the Indian River, Captain Sharpe. Sharpe wrote a letter to Henry Flagler

explaining that his grove had been ruined. After Henry
made sure that Sharpe really needed his help, he gave
him a loan. The men agreed that the farmer would
pay Henry back when his next orange crop was sold.
Captain Sharpe was very grateful for the help. When
his new orange crop was ready for market, he invited
Henry to visit. They enjoyed each other's company and
became good friends. When it came time to repay the
loan, Henry would not take the money. Every winter
after that, for the rest of Captain Sharpe's life, some of
his delicious citrus fruit was sent to his friend Henry
Flagler. This was a way to say "thank you" for Henry's
gift.

There was one person farther south who hoped
that the freezes in northern and central Florida would
help her cause. Julia D. Tuttle lived in Miami, a small
settlement that had grown up around old Fort Dallas.
Fort Dallas was a fort built by soldiers during the
Seminole Indian Wars years before. Julia Tuttle wanted
Henry Flagler to bring his railroad to her area.

Mrs. Tuttle had asked him many times by letter,
but his answer had always been "no." He had been
too busy north of Miami. After the severe freeze,
however, Henry thought again about taking his railroad
farther south. When he learned that the frost had not

reached Mrs. Tuttle's town, Mr. Flagler and his business advisers took a boat trip to see Miami for themselves.

Sure enough, the citrus trees in the Miami area were loaded with fresh fruit. Flagler was delighted again by the beauty of a settlement along Florida's east coast. Only a few houses overlooked such a magnificent view. The surf of the Atlantic Ocean crashed against the sandy shore. The Miami River bubbled over rapids into blue-green Biscayne Bay. Tall Royal Palms were everywhere. Flagler liked what he saw. His advisers spoke with some of the settlers. The residents told them that they would be very happy to have one of Mr. Flagler's grand hotels!

Julia Tuttle and others wanted a smooth-riding, efficient railroad line to connect them with Northern states. That way any land that she and her neighbors owned would be worth much more money. Mrs. Tuttle even promised to give Mr. Flagler some of her own land to be used for the hotel and railroad terminal. William Brickell also offered land. He had run an Indian trading post there for years.

Before he went to bed on the first night of his visit, Flagler had already made up his mind. He would bring his railroad to the shores of Biscayne Bay. He would also build another magnificent hotel. This one he would name the Hotel Royal Palm.

Reaching Miami by a land route would be another challenge. There were about sixty-five miles of unexplored forests and swamps between Palm Beach and Miami. There were trees that were very difficult to cut down, even with the sharpest axe. The woods were so thick that mail was even delivered in a special way. It had to be taken either by boat or by a mailman who walked along the sandy coastline to reach the settlement.

A painting showing a mailman walking along the Atlantic Ocean in south Florida. *(Courtesy of the State Archives of Florida)*

Chapter 8

Off to Miami!

In September of 1895, Henry Flagler's railroad was re-named the Florida East Coast Railway. By this time, his railroad lines covered most of the eastern coast of Florida.

The Hotel Royal Palm was spectacular. It was built on fifteen beautiful acres, with swaying palm trees surrounding the building. From the balconies, guests could see the Miami River, Biscayne Bay, and Florida's Everglades. As soon as the railroad was completed to the area, visitors started filling the hotel rooms.

Like other towns, Miami grew very quickly when the Florida East Coast Railway arrived. Mr. Flagler again helped to build up the town. His workers paved streets, and they built churches and schools. He brought electric light to people who had not seen it before. He built a dock for large ships coming from Cuba and

The first passenger Florida East Coast Railway train into Miami, Florida, 1896. (Courtesy of the State Archives of Florida)

South America, as well as Northern cities. People came into town faster than builders could construct homes for them. Soon the tiny settlement of Miami became a city.

To show their appreciation, some of the townspeople wanted to change the name of the town to "Flagler," but Henry didn't want them to do that. He wanted them to keep the Indian name "Miami," which means "sweet water." Years later, though, Miami was still called "the city that Flagler built."

Flagler had been building hotels and railroads along the east coast of Florida. Soon he would have another home for himself as well. In 1901, after a divorce from his second wife, Henry married a young woman named Mary Lily Kenan. He built a large home for his new wife in Palm Beach, near the Hotel Royal Poinciana. They named it Whitehall.

Mary Lily and Henry Flagler's home in Palm Beach, Whitehall.
(© Flagler Museum Archives)

Henry Flagler and Mary Lily Kenan Flagler. (© *Flagler Museum Archives*)

By that time, Henry Flagler was more than seventy years old. He had already spent millions of dollars in the state of Florida. Surely, after reaching Miami, he was ready to retire at last! After all, his railroad line nearly reached the southern tip of the state. And he had built many beautiful hotels from St. Augustine to Miami.

Yet Henry Flagler still saw things to be done. There was a large city at the end of the Florida Keys that also wanted to be connected by railroad to the rest of the state. Key West was a bigger city than Miami at this time, and it had a deep sea port. That port allowed ocean-going ships to easily bring trade from South and Central America or Cuba. Also, the United States government was planning to build the Panama Canal. Key West could be used to protect the Canal.

Building track between Daytona and Miami over land had been difficult, but this would be the challenge of Flagler's lifetime. Others had considered it earlier, but a railroad across the Keys was never built. Flagler and his advisors talked with many experts about the idea. He wanted to make sure they knew every detail of the job. As always, Mr. Flagler had to be sure the project could be completed, and completed properly. Along the Keys, the workmen would not be building

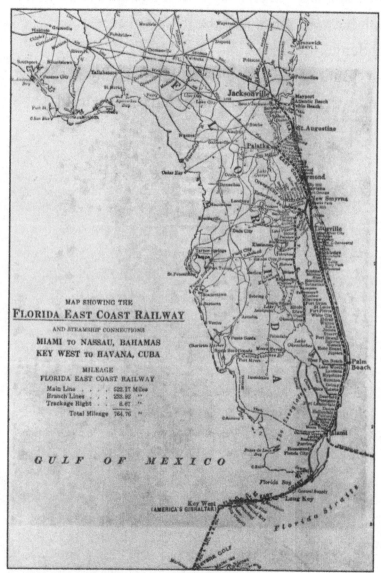

Map showing the Florida East Coast Railway, from Jacksonville to Key West. (Courtesy of the State Archives of Florida)

track on land, but on rough coral islands and on bridges built between those islands. It was an enormous challenge.

But to Henry Flagler, building a railroad to Key West was something else he could do for Florida.

Chapter 9

Rolling into Key West

Again, a decision was made. Work on a railroad built over land and sea started in the summer of 1905. Henry Flagler's engineers had the information they thought they needed even before they laid the first rail. They had studied how high the waves might get, even in bad weather. They felt sure they could keep the track safe. They had studied the force of winds that might hit the Keys, even in a hurricane. And they had plans on how to build a bridge that was *seven miles* long.

All of their information and plans couldn't solve everything, however. They still ran into all kinds of unexpected problems. Every step of the way they met with new challenges.

The men worked for seven long years. Slowly but surely, railroad track was built across more than thirty islands. The track connected south Florida to Key West.

At times there were as many as 3,000 men working in extremely hot weather. They were constantly troubled by mosquitoes, alligators, snakes, and even hurricane-force winds.

Three large hurricanes hit the islands while they were working. The hurricane of 1906 was the worst. The high winds blew some of the workmen out to sea and many lives were lost. Henry's engineers learned from each storm and each major challenge. They learned more lessons about the weather and how to keep their men and the track safe.

With each crisis, Henry Flagler realized again that he had chosen the best engineers to do this awesome job. He was sure they had taken the best possible care of the workmen and that they would eventually succeed. When he reached the age of eighty, however, he just hoped he would live long enough to see it finished. His engineers hoped so too.

They did it! Just after Henry's eighty-second birthday, the workers finished the track. Henry Flagler and other railroad officials were on the first official train that rolled across the Keys and into Key West. The date was January 22, 1912.

About 10,000 people were waiting at the station. They loudly cheered and celebrated the event. Some

The Florida East Coast Railway's first arrival in Key West, January 22, 1912. (Courtesy of the State Archives of Florida)

of these people had always lived on Key West and had never seen a passenger train before!

Henry Flagler had done so much for Florida. His Florida East Coast Railway stretched from Jacksonville to Key West. It could go no farther. He owned grand hotels and had built up cities along the coast. He had completed even more than he set out to do, and he was tired.

On May 20, 1913, Henry Flagler died. It had been a little more than a year since the triumphant ride into Key West. He was eighty-three years old. Henry was laid to rest at Memorial Presbyterian Church in St. Augustine. He was buried near his first wife Mary, his daughter Jennie Louise, and her baby.

This man had made a promise to himself when he was young. He kept that promise. He also opened up a whole state so that others might also enjoy Florida. He made millions, and he spent millions. He seemed to enjoy the whole challenge of his life. His adventures have become part of Florida's exciting history.

Henry Morrison Flagler portrait. Date unknown. (Courtesy of the State Archives of Florida)

Afterword

Henry Morrison Flagler's name is remembered in
many places along Florida's east coast. There is a
Flagler County, and a city called Flagler Beach. Streets,
libraries, and schools have been named for him too.
The beautiful Hotel Ponce de Leon is no longer a hotel.
Now it is Flagler College. Whitehall, the Flaglers' home
in Palm Beach, is now The Henry Morrison Flagler
Museum. It's a wonderful place to visit.

Henry Flagler's railroads allowed many people
to visit or move to Florida. Miami's growth is a good
example. Before the arrival of the railroad, there were
only 726 people in what is now called Miami-Dade
County. Soon after the railroad arrived, there were more
than five times as many people. By 1913, the year that
Flagler died, Miami was the fifth-largest city in Florida.

The Florida East Coast Railway is still in business
today. However, it no longer runs from Miami to Key

West. A hurricane in 1935 did a lot of damage in the Keys, and the decision was made not to rebuild the railroad track. Instead, a roadway was paved for automobile traffic. But if you travel that route today, you can still see some of the railroad track built years ago by Henry Flagler's workmen.

Henry Flagler appreciated the money he had made in business in the North. He spent that money in a Southern state where he could make a difference. He needed a huge challenge, and Florida was ready for his creative mind and his ideas. Thirty years later, he left the state much changed from the way he found it.

Henry Morrison Flagler was determined to overcome any challenge, big or small. And he did. When he was fourteen he walked nine miles to a boat that would take him to a new job. At age eighty, he was still working hard to build up a state. Henry always planned ahead to succeed. Even when he had millions to spend, he never forgot what it was like to be poor. Throughout his life he kept that little French coin he had with him when he arrived in Ohio for his first job away from home. He kept it as a reminder of his past. Henry Morrison Flagler, builder of Florida, can be an inspiration to us all.

Places to Visit

• The Henry Morrison Flagler Museum (Whitehall, once the home
of the Flaglers)
    One Whitehall Way
    P. O. Box 969
    Palm Beach, FL 33480
    Website: www.flaglermuseum.us
    Phone: 561-655-2833
Henry Flagler's private railroad car is on the grounds.

• Flagler College (once the Hotel Ponce de Leon)
    P. O. Box 1027
    St. Augustine, FL 32085
    Website: www.flagler.edu
    Phone: 904-829-6481

Glossary

adventurous – daring, willing to take chances

alert – to be aware of what is happening, paying attention

climate – temperature and weather in a place

convince – to talk a person into believing what you are saying

construct – to build

elegant – well-made, beautiful

extend – to go further

invest – to put money into a project you believe in, which you expect to later bring more money to you in return

luxury – more than what is needed, a treat

magnificent – very beautiful, very special, awesome

pleasant – comfortable, nice

port – where ships come in, a harbor

refining oil – making oil purer

retire – to stop working for a living

settlement – a place where people make their homes

stage coach – a four-wheeled carriage pulled by horses

thriving – healthy, growing

terminus – the end of a railroad line

transportation – the way by which people or things
      move from one place to another, as in a train or car

unreliable – not to be depended upon

triumphant – a happy feeling when something is done

tropical – a warm climate or a description of plants that
      live in a warm climate

Bibliography

Akin, Edward N. *Flagler: Rockefeller Partner and Florida Baron.*
Gainesville, FL: University Press of Florida, 1991.

Bramson, Seth H. *Speedway to Sunshine: the Story of the Florida
East Coast Railway.* Erin, Ontario, Canada: Boston Mills
Press, 2003.

Chandler, David Leon. *Henry Flagler: The Astonishing Life and
Times of the Visionary Robber Baron Who Founded Florida.*
New York: Macmillan, 1986.

Martin, Sidney Walter. *Florida's Flagler.* Athens, GA: The
University of Georgia Press, 1949.

Sammons, Sandra Wallus. *The Two Henrys: Henry Plant and Henry
Flagler and Their Railroads.* Sarasota, FL: Pineapple Press,
2010.

References

Note: "Ibid." is short for the Latin word *ibidem*, which means "in the same place." Below, if you see "ibid.," that means a quote came from the same book as the quote before it did.

After the Dedication.
"I have always been contented, but I have never been satisfied. . ." Edward N. Akin, *Flagler: Rockefeller Partner and Florida Baron* (Gainesville, FL: University Press of Florida, 1991), 230.

Chapter 1
Page 6. "We worked night and day. . ." David Leon Chandler, *Henry Flagler: The Astonishing Life and Times of the Visionary Robber Baron who Founded Florida* (New York: Macmillan, 1986), 60.

Chapter 3
Page 10. "For about fourteen or fifteen years. . ." Sidney Walter Martin, *Florida's Flagler* (Athens, GA: The University of Georgia Press, 1949), 115.

Chapter 6
Page 15. "Flagler Alerts." Ibid., 143.

Chapter 8
Page 19. ". . .the city that Flagler built." Ibid., 150.

Acknowledgments

Many thanks to John M. Blades, Executive Director of the Flagler Museum in Palm Beach; David Carson, Public Affairs Director at the Flagler Museum; and Amanda Wilson, Public Affairs Department Assistant at the Flagler Museum.

Thanks go out as well to to Thomas Graham, Professor of History Emeritus, Flagler College, St. Augustine, and to Seth H. Bramson, Company Historian, Florida East Coast Railway, and Adjunct Professor of History at Barry University and Florida International University, as well as the author of fourteen books on local south Florida and state transportation history.

In Charlotte County Public Schools, much appreciation to: Donna Dunakey, Curriculum and Instruction Specialist, Social Sciences PreK-12; Sandra Rink, Fourth Grade Teacher, Deep Creek Elementary; Nancy Ehrnsberger, Fourth Grade Teacher, Liberty Elementary. In Sarasota County Public Schools: Ms. Lois Collins, Fourth Grade Teacher, Englewood Elementary; Students Gracie Helbing, Emily McCarty, Dakota

Johnson, and Todd Park. Also many thanks to Phyllis Lewis and Bob Sammons.

Thanks to Nina McGuire, a very dear friend and the publisher of the first edition of this work. Thanks as well to David and June Cussen of Pineapple Press, who realized the need for a new edition, and to Heather Waters for her editorial assistance.

Thanks to the many librarians—especially at the Elsie Quirk Library in Englewood, Florida—who have been so helpful with my many inter-library loan requests.

Index

(Numbers in **bold** refer to photographs.)

About the Author

Sandra Wallus Sammons moved from Pennsylvania
to Florida and became fascinated with the Sunshine
State's history. As an elementary school librarian in
Lake County, Florida, she learned of the need for books
on Florida's history on a fourth-grade reading level. She
began writing biographies of fascinating Floridians.
So many lived such inspirational lives. She now lives
in central Florida with her husband and their black cat,
Spades.

Here are some other books from Pineapple Press on related topics. For a complete catalog, visit our website at www.pineapplepress.com. Or write to Pineapple Press, P.O. Box 3889, Sarasota, Florida 34230-3889, or call (800) 746-3275.

Also by Sandra Wallus Sammons

The Two Henrys: Henry Plant and Henry Flagler and Their Railroads. Henry Plant and Henry Flagler changed the landscape of Florida in the late 1800s and early 1900s. This dual biography is a story of railroads and the men who built them with their creativity, innovation, and money. Flagler opened up the east coast of Florida with his railroads and hotels, and Plant did the same on the west coast of the state. Ages 12 and up.

Marjory Stoneman Douglas and the Florida Everglades. Marjory Stoneman Douglas is called "the grandmother of the Everglades." Read about her life from her childhood up north to her long and inspiring life in south Florida. When she arrived in Miami in 1915 she began to understand the importance of the Everglades, an area most people considered a "swamp." She called attention to it in her book *Everglades: River of Grass.* During her 108 years, she was a newspaper and magazine journalist as well as a book writer. She received the Presidential Medal of Freedom for her work on the Everglades. Ages 9–12.

Marjorie Kinnan Rawlings and the Florida Crackers. Marjorie Kinnan Rawlings grew up loving to write and hoping to become an author. Later she moved to Florida, where she lived out in the country at Cross Creek near an area called the Big Scrub. She met the people who lived there, the so-called Crackers. Their simple way of life fascinated her, so she wrote stories about them. One of her books, called *The Yearling*, was about a boy and his pet deer. This book won the Pulitzer Prize for fiction. Her dream of becoming a famous writer had come true. Ages 9–12.

Other Young Reader Titles from Pineapple Press

The Young Naturalist's Guide to Florida, Second Edition, by Peggy Sias Lantz and Wendy A. Hale. Newly updated. This enticing book shows you where and how to look for Florida's most interesting natural features and creatures. Take it along on your next walk in the woods.

Everglades: An Ecosystem Facing Choices and Challenges by Anne E. Ake. The Everglades is like no other place in the world. Its shallow, slowly flowing waters create an ecosystem of mysterious beauty with a great diversity of plant and animal life. But the Everglades ecosystem is in trouble. Learn about what's being done to help and why the Everglades are worth saving.

Escape to the Everglades by Edwina Raffa and Annelle Rigsby. Fiction. Based on historical fact, this young adult novel tells the story of Will Cypress, a half-Seminole boy living among his mother's people during the Second Seminole War. He meets Chief Osceola and travels with him to St. Augustine. Ages 9–14.

Kidnapped in Key West by Edwina Raffa and Annelle Rigsby. Fiction. Twelve-year-old Eddie Malone is living in the Florida Keys in 1912 when suddenly his world is turned upside down. His father, a worker on Henry Flagler's Over-Sea Railroad, is thrown into jail for stealing the railroad payroll. Eddie is determined to prove his father's innocence. But then the real thieves kidnap Eddie. Can he escape? Well he ever get home? Will he be able to prove Pa's innocence? Ages 8–12.

The Treasure of Amelia Island by M.C. Finotti. Fiction. Mary Kingsley, the youngest child of former slave Ana Jai Kingsley, recounts the life-changing events of December 1813. Her family lives in La Florida, a Spanish territory under siege by Patriots who see no place for freed people of color in a new Florida. Against these mighty events, Mary decides to search for a legendary pirate treasure with her brothers. Ages 8–12.

The Spy Who Came In from the Sea by Peggy Nolan. Fiction. In 1943 fourteen-year-old Frank Holleran sees an enemy spy land on Jacksonville Beach. First Frank needs to get people to believe him, and then he needs to stop the spy from carrying out his dangerous plans. Winner of the Sunshine State Young Reader's Award. Ages 8–12.

Florida Lighthouses for Kids by Elinor DeWire. Learn why some lighthouses are tall and some short, why a cat parachuted off St. Augustine Lighthouse, and much more. Lots of color pictures. Ages 9 and up.

The Florida Quiz Book: How Much Do You Know about Florida? by Hollee Temple. More than 2,500 questions and answers on topics like agriculture, architecture, art, the economy, ecosystems, the environment, plants, animals, geology, geography, history, the Keys, law, literature, meteorology, the oceans and coastline, parks, space science, and good-old, general Florida statistics.

CPSIA information can be obtained
at www.ICGtesting.com
Printed in the USA
BVOW09s2232231117
500744BV00001B/3/P